MY GRIEF, MY JOY

My Grief, My Joy

Kenn Edwards

First Printing, 2026

ISBN 979-8-9887782-9-5

ISBN (Ebook) 979-8-9887782-8-8

www.runewalker.com

Kenn Edwards

PO Box 188

Stockton, Utah

84071

USA

CONTENTS

To my beautiful baby boy, Henry.
You brought me so much
joy and love.
I miss you!!!

MY BABY BOY

Henry is my baby boy.

One day in June 2012, I received a message from a friend about an adorable little Chihuahua up for adoption. He was approximately eight months old and had come to Portland from California through a second-chance program. My partner and I took our other two dogs to meet him and see how they got along with him. Our other two dogs were bigger and also slightly anxious being at the adoption center, but Henry tried to play with them anyway. They were too overwhelmed to play, but showed that they didn't mind him. So, we brought him home.

I thought I would have more time with him. Fourteen years is a long time, though. We had a few close calls with him over the years, and I am grateful they were only close calls.

On March 25, 2026, Henry fell asleep in my arms for the last time. I buried him out back and visit him every day.

My mom passed away in 2020, and that was difficult for me. Losing Henry was a whole different experience. He was my baby boy. He was my shadow. We were together every day. He was definitely my truest companion. I was, and am still, afraid that I will forget him. That led me to what is now this celebration of him. Even now, I have had to stop typing to cry and wipe snot from my nose several times.

I miss my baby boy. I am grateful you have chosen to take a little time to witness my grief and my joy. I hope your time with us inspires you to remember your own loves lost and even to take the chance on love again.

FRIES

I gave in
    it's my fault
I dare anyone to resist
Ok maybe I'm not
the only one to blame
and I'm sure as hell
not the only one
to give in

you love french fries
sometimes I would have
to get all of the salt off
before you could eat them

you have selective smelling
and would wait until
I sat down to eat
before ignoring your
custom-made food

you love the smell of
french fries
and know
I'm bringing them home
from miles away
I upsized my order
to share with you

it's weird
I'm sure
that I bite off small
pieces of fry for you

somehow you know
or maybe you've trained me
that we're done when I say
"Ok, that's the last one"

I'm picky about my fries
I like them hot
and firm
and just the right amount
of salt
You
aren't as picky

today
as in the past week
I ordered fries
to bring home
to share with you
no matter the drive-thru
no matter the day
my throat
my nose
my eyes
are overwhelmed
are surprised
by the
tidal wave
from my heart

aftershocks
from the day
my heart broke

I still bite
the fries
into small pieces
for you
I lay them
on your resting place
instead of at my feet

I long desperately
for your silent
patient
stare
waiting for fries

ONE WEEK

Today
        approximately 175 hours or
10,500 minutes or
630,000 seconds
after your last breath
I worry that
I will forget you
that completing
my daily tasks
is a distraction
that leads to
forgetting
you

I was told once
years ago
"grief and sadness
validate the love lost"

what does it mean
when those moments of
"grief and sadness"
become
less intense
fewer

does that mean...

I don't even want
to think
to say
to pen
the possible answers
that end with a period
following words like
I've
Forgotten
You

or
I've
Grown
Accustom
To
Your Absence

right now
every sentence
begins and ends
with
tears and
sniffling

I feel
the grip
lessening
with each passing
day
hour
second

how do I hold
knuckle-white
to you
your presence
your love

are we built to do that

each day
I return
home
to the missing
sounds
smells
to the missing
dance to go for a walk
to the missing
Bark
that insists on some cat food
to empty blankets
to your hoodie
to your unused food bowl

is it betrayal
that those moments
are shorter
that I can scroll
past them with less time spent
but not without
heartache
quickened breath
hand to my mouth
hand to my heart
holding me together

you held me together
I held you
but you held me
together

I have no idea
how to lose you
how to not plan
my days around you
how to not make
sure you get just
a little cat food

how to not make sure
you're warm enough

I pled to the land
to hold you tight
and warm
to keep you safe

I'm a visitor now
each visit
starting
and
ending
with tears

RUMBLE STRIPS

Day 9
  I went to the city to see a show
an early birthday present
although I'd rather have you

I thought of you
one thought
encompasses
a decade or more
of our time together
and can be summed up
in one experience
Rumble Strips

you hated them
sometimes they are
unavoidable
sometimes I'm a bad driver

tonight during the show
the performer had a
magic trick
that culminated with
"you are right where
you are meant to be"

tears came immediately
and faded as quickly
(I was in public, ya know)
I thought of you

we were meant to be
adventurers
travelers
together
but you hate my car

It's a very compact car
with two doors and a hatchback
needless to say
Rumble Strips
are amplified
and all sounds and vibrations
are unmuffled

the moment
wheels touch strips
you would leap
into my lap
there's not much room
for a 6-foot tall human
and you
but we got semi-comfortable

every time I drive over
Rumble Strips
I remember
trying to make you stay
in your seat

Foolish
all of those moments
Foolish

I'd give anything
to have you
leap into my lap
just one more time

your other parent
would try to coach me
on making the car
comfortable for you

he wasn't wrong
but you know I am
only surpassed in
stubbornness
by you

at least with kids
they grow to an age
where one can try
to reason with them

my Chihuahua,
you stayed
or
grew
more stubborn with the years

I should have known that
naming you
Henry
and calling you
King Henry
would lead to
champagne tastes
I wish I had a
champagne budget
to match
the love and happiness
that you brought me

on our journey together
your passing was calm
you drifted off to sleep
no Rumble Strips

I
on the other hand
have never had more
Rumble Strips

(slow down)

RUN OR WALK

Yesterday
        I took my first walk
without you

fourteen years ago
we walked the trails
on the Columbia River
you wanted to keep up
with the big dogs
I had to tie a fifty-foot
fluorescent orange cord
to your harness

so I could step on it
to stop you

I'm glad I did
I remember you diving
into the Sandy River
following Gus and Cody
(the big dogs)
you swam after them
until there was no more cord
it almost acted like a spring
turning you around
swimming back to us
on the shore

come back to me now

I like to think
we are cut from the
same clothe
we were both
runners
in our youth

I chased you down
the street
more times than I can
count

one trip to the beach
was very memorable
three adults
four dogs
the reenactment would be
a truly epic
performance piece
one brief stop turned into a
veritable blockbuster action movie
filled with
harrowing rescues
bloody combat
(with the pavement)
chase sequences
and graceful barrel rolls

I'm not sure how
you and I both avoided
the traffic
as I chased you onto the busy highway
but we made it

for a time
we had a dog door
and fenced yard
you loved that
freedom

I loved our walks
you always wanted
to wander longer
than I did
or longer than
the time I had allotted
because of work
or some other thing
that took me from home
and you

I'm sure you needed
a break
a nap

at home
you
were my shadow
unless I had been in
your
seat too long

on your last day
we took a long walk
we followed our usual route

you had so much
life
your whole life
right up until
the long nap

I saw today
a friend's post that said
something like
dogs don't say
goodbye
they just run ahead
and wait for us to
catch up

Henry
Don't get too far ahead

TWO WEEKS

Two Weeks Tomorrow
    it's also my birthday
betcha can't guess
what I really want

I do ok
I haven't made any sort of
announcement
I'm not ready to
talk much about you
I can't without sobbing
Fuck
I can't write this without tears

I do ok
until
I get ready to leave work early
and I think
"Oh, we have enough daylight
to take a walk"

I do ok
until
I think about stopping
for dinner
and automatically
plan to order
fries and roast beef
for you

I do ok
until
I walk past
your food crumbs
still on the floor

I just can't
clean it up

I do ok
until
I open the fridge
and see the pumpkin
I put in your food
or
I see your food
on top of the fridge

I do ok
when
I'm distracted

I think we all do OK
when we are distracted

I don't want to be
distracted
into numbness
into forgetting

I swear that
last night
I heard
your little growl
telling me to get up and move

I swear that
I felt
you sitting on the floor
near me
waiting for a walk

I'm not ok
I cry
I miss you

I am not Ok
I wasn't ready
but who is ever ready
to see their
Everything
go

you were the
one
living being
who factored into
every decision
I made

there is freedom
in having that
and
not having that

freedom
doesn't feel like
freedom

BETRAYAL

I feel like it's a
    betrayal
to feel happy
without you here

you don't feel
that way
I know

I misassign emotions
while grasping at
straws
because
you are not here
to hold

my love
I miss you

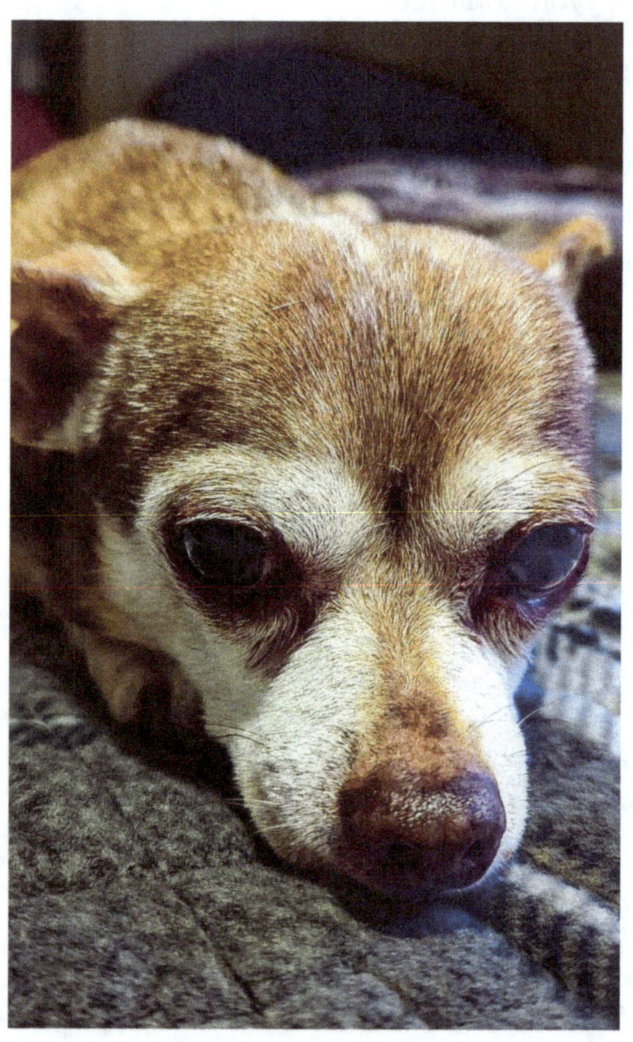

SCARS

Love is
apparently
a battlefield

a year and a half ago
I found myself
in the ER
getting stitches

you were in a lot of
pain
we spent two days
visiting the vet

figuring out
what was going on with you

I believe it was
arthritis
and
it's possible you
were just pissed off
because I wouldn't give
you cheetos
like your other dad
with whom
you had just spent
some months
(no shade)

that was the first
well no
the second time
I mourned your death
while you were still alive

I had that wound
opened and reopened
and reopened
that scar
is on my heart
I'm having a
difficult time
keeping it closed now
it reopens whenever
you
come to mind

my stitches
sealed up two
openings on my brow
from your
sharp teeth

they healed up nicely
the other wound may not
I can still see
them if I look closely

I was almost
elated
to have it happen
it meant having
something
to look at
anytime
anywhere
and that would
remind me
of
you

FLOOR

You won't care
    it's been almost
three weeks
and I have
not
cleaned up the
floor where you ate

I'm still unsure
why
you stopped eating
from your
or any

dish
and why
you had to eat
off of the floor

I know
or fear
that cleaning the floor
will be
too final

I started collecting
things that could
be donated
doggie bags
food

I will not get rid of
your blankets
or hoodies

My words and thoughts
seem to be dancing
on the edge of
tears
but are held
back by my mind
trying to
put words together
to form some sort of
meaning
some sort of
connection
I feel that dancing
on this precipice
will cause insanity

I am becoming
aware
of how I am
speaking to
you
and
other animals
when I am

alone
of course
I think of
the so-called
mad/insane folks
of the past
maybe they lost
someone
like I have lost you

I'm not opposed to
living in the wilds
talking to the
animals
trees
winds
but you will still
be gone

PROOF?

As I come to write this final piece, I think that phrase, "Grief is Proof of Love," might be incorrect, or at least too few letters to describe something indescribable by words. Merriam-Webster uses the word

distress
which deals with pain and suffering
those seem to be side effects of
something more
Loss is tossed around as a descriptor
the only four-letter word that returns

again and again and again
to my lips is
miss

I miss you

I miss you waking me up to go outside
I miss you taking up most of the bed
I miss you cuddling with me

I miss you

I miss you flopping into me
I miss you waking me up to feed you
I miss you pretending to want to go
outside just so I would get up from the
spot you wanted to sit in

I miss you

I miss your sass
I miss your protection
I miss your stare when I had food

I miss you

I miss your happy, excited spin
I miss your sunbathing blissfully
I miss coming home to you

I miss you

I miss you as my shadow
I miss your kisses
I miss hearing the tip-tap rhythm of
your nails on the tile floor as you ran to
greet me every time I came home

I miss you

I wish I had a recording of your nails on
the tile floor

I long so deeply to hear that
just once more

and I never will

I miss you

I love you
my baby boy

GRATITUDE

Thank you for sharing this
     celebration of joy and grief
with me
may this be a source of
Joy
Grief
connection
companionship
solace
hope
tears
chuckles
and so much more

I'm so sorry for all of your loss
may you have witness
may you have support
may you have proof of Love
in more than Grief
in a life well-lived and loved

Kenn was Henry's human companion.

Among many labels, Kenn is an author, podcast host, psychic medium, teacher, photographer, shaman, and rune walker of the Northern Tradition, with roots in Norse and Anglo-Saxon Paganisms.

Kenn works to facilitate the liberation of the wise, untamed, and passionate being within those he works with through his podcasts, writings, classes, and one-on-one sessions.